DATE DUE

SEP 22 1975	MAY 11 2002		
DEC 13	1	FEB 0 8 2007	
FEB 3		MAR 0 1 2007	
JUL 18		MAR 2 1 2007	
OCT. 25 1983			
MAR. 1985			
JUN 1986			
AUG 2 2 1986			
MAR 2 1987			
MAR 2 8			
DEC 1 1989			
SEP 27 1990			
JUL 2 2001			
DEC 3 1 2001			

GAYLORD   PRINTED IN U.S.A.

About the Book

John Muir loved the wild beauty and freedom of nature from the time he was a little boy in Scotland. As a grown man in America, he walked thousands of miles in the wilderness. Perhaps his favorite of all the places he saw was the Yosemite Valley in California. As a shepherd, Muir came to know each of its mountainsides and waterfalls. In later years, John Muir wrote stories about nature. He explained why and how the wilderness should be saved. Because of what he said, Yosemite Valley and many other beautiful places are preserved as national parks, for all to enjoy.

The Author-Artist

GLEN DINES has written or illustrated well over a dozen children's books, most of them telling the history of the American frontiers. Mr. Dines was educated at the University of Washington in Seattle and at the Art Center School in Los Angeles. He has been a free-lance artist in New York and a staff artist on the Pacific edition of *Stars and Stripes* in Tokyo. Previously, he wrote and illustrated *Crazy Horse* and *Sun, Sand, and Steel* for Putnam.

JOHN MUIR

A SEE AND READ Biography

written and illustrated by

GLEN DINES

G. P. Putnam's Sons • New York

Text and illustrations copyright © 1974 by Glen Dines
All rights reserved.
SBN: GB-399-60880-X
SBN: TR-399-20390-7
Library of Congress Catalog Card Number: 73-87217
PRINTED IN THE UNITED STATES OF AMERICA

"Please, Mother," John Muir
said, "it's Saturday. The other
boys are going over to the old castle!"

"No!" John's mother said. "You
play in the garden with your
brother David. You are not to
run wild."

Mrs. Muir went inside the house.

But John ran to the garden wall.

"Father will whip you when he comes home!" John's little brother said.

"I know," John said. "But being in this little garden all day is worse than any whipping."

John climbed over the wall. He

and his friends ran down the
streets of the Scottish town of
Dunbar. They ran across the
fields of a farmer. They ran
through the farmer's hedges.

"You rascals!" the angry
farmer shouted. "Go back to the
town where you belong!"

The boys ran until they came
to Old Dunbar Castle. The walls
were crumbling, but John climbed
to the top. He saw dark
clouds. "A storm is coming!"
he shouted.

After a while the other boys went
home, but John walked along the
shore. He listened to the wind. He
watched the waves crash against the
black rocks. John was happy. He
felt wild and free.

Later John walked home in the rain.
His mother was angry. "Wait
until your father comes home!"
she said.

But when John's father came home, he did not give John a whipping. Instead he said, "Get ready, John. You are going to America tomorrow!"

John knew his father had been planning to become a preacher in the New World.

"I will take David and sister
Sarah, too," John's father said.
  "The others must stay here until we
find a place to live in America."
  John was sad to leave his mother
and sisters and brothers.

But he was excited, too. John
had read books about America. It
was a wilderness where great
flocks of birds filled the sky.
People said there were trees filled with
sugar and rivers filled with gold.

It took six long weeks to sail
across the Atlantic Ocean to
America. John and David played on
the deck every day. Poor Sarah
was seasick. She stayed in bed
most of the time.

Once in the United States, they
rode on trains, riverboats, and
steamboats. They saw places with
strange sounding names: Michigan,
Minnesota, Milwaukee.

Finally they came to their new
home in Wisconsin. It was a tiny

cabin in the middle of a great
forest. Everything was new and
strange.

John missed his mother and
sisters and brothers and friends
in faraway Scotland. But there
was much to see and do in the
woods.

He saw flocks of passenger
pigeons, like great rivers in the
sky. He learned how to get sugar
by cutting notches in the trunks
of maple trees.

"The forest is like a beautiful
book," John said to himself. "I
want to read every page."

John helped his father build a
bigger house. In the fall John's
mother and his sisters and
brothers traveled to America. At
last the family was together
again. But with so many
mouths to feed, everyone had to
work hard.

John cleared fields. He plowed
and planted. He split logs to

make fences. He worked from
morning until night.

Still John found time to read.
He read his father's Bible. He
walked many miles to borrow books
from his neighbors. John read the
books at night, after supper.
"If I could wake up very early in
the morning," John thought, "I'd
have more time to read."

So John made a clocklike machine out of pieces of hickory wood. "This is my early-rising machine," John said. "It tells time, rings a bell in the morning, and even shakes my bed."

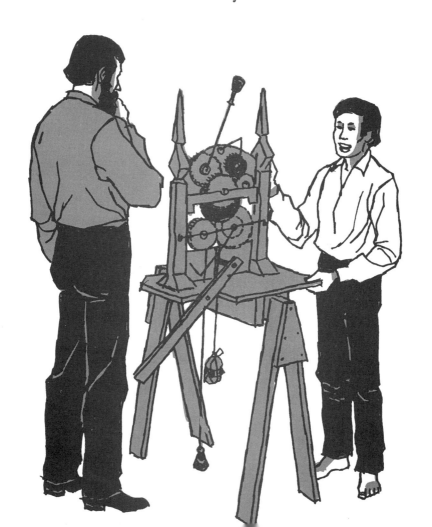

When he had no books to read, John made machines instead. He made a machine that fed the horses. He made a thermometer as tall as himself.

John made a big clock. He put it on the top of the barn.

"John!" his father shouted. "People are coming from miles around to see your clock. They are frightening our chickens and cows. You must take the clock down!"

When John was twenty-one years old, he said good-bye to his father and mother. "I must find my own life," he said. He took three machines with him. "Perhaps I can sell these." He rode on a train to a big city. He asked the engineer if he could ride on the front of the train. The man smiled and said yes.

There was a fair in the city.
John showed his machines. The
people crowded around to see John's
machines. They gave John a prize.

The fair was near the University
of Wisconsin. John saw all the

books in the library. "If only I could go to school here!" he said. "But I don't have much money."

"If you work hard all summer," a student said, "you can earn enough money to stay in school the rest of the year. Why don't you ask the president of the university?"

John was nervous, but he went to the president anyway. John told the man about his schooling in Scotland, his reading, and his machines.

"Yes," the president said. "You can come to school here."

John was happy. He read all the books about mountains and trees and flowers. He made a desk that opened and closed the books so he could read faster.

He made a bed that stood him on his feet in the morning.

Soon John's room was filled with machines. Even the president of the university came to see John's machines.

After four years, John left the
university. He worked in a
factory making wagon wheels.

One day a piece of metal flew
into John's eye. John fell
backward, covering his eyes with
his hands. When he took his hands
away, he saw only blackness!

John was blind for many weeks. But later he could see again.

"I've been given a second chance!" John said. "I must see all the trees and flowers I read about in the university."

John stopped working. He started
walking with only a compass, a
small bag of clothes, and a press
made of flat pieces of wood tied
together. John collected plants
and flowers and kept them between
the pieces of wood.

John walked 1,000 miles from
Indiana to Florida. Sometimes he
went hungry and cold. But he was
happy. He remembered the time he
walked along the shore near
old Dunbar Castle. "I am wild and
free again!" John told himself.

John remembered a book he had
read about a place in faraway
California—a valley called
Yosemite. "It is in the Sierra
Nevada," John remembered.
"It has great trees and waterfalls
and mountains of solid stone.
There is no other place like it
in the world.

"I must see this wonderful
place!" John said to himself.

John sailed to San Francisco, a city in California. Once ashore, he stopped the first person he saw. "Where is the valley called Yosemite?" John asked.

Surprised, the man only pointed. John walked in that direction.

John walked along the San
Francisco Bay. He crossed some
small mountains. He came to a
wide valley filled with wild
flowers.

"This is like wading in a river of blossoms," John said to himself. He could see tall, snow-covered mountains in the distance. He knew they were the Sierra Nevada.

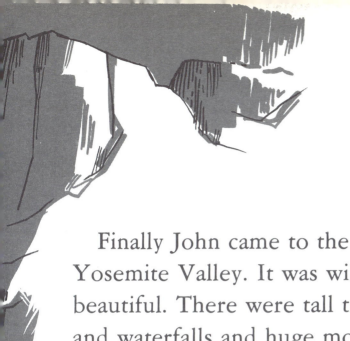

Finally John came to the
Yosemite Valley. It was wild and
beautiful. There were tall trees
and waterfalls and huge mountains
of stone.

John wanted to see everything.
He worked as a sheepherder so he
could stay in the mountains.

One night John climbed high on
the rock behind a waterfall. "The
moon looks as if it is swimming,"
John thought. But the water fell
hard and fast. It fell on John.
He climbed down quickly.

One time John climbed a tall
tree during a windstorm. The
tree bent this way and that. John
held on tightly and listened to
the music of the wind.

John walked alone in the mountains. He carried only a blanket, a tin cup, and a sack filled with tea, sugar, and bread. At night he slept on the ground.

Once a famous scientist came to Yosemite. "This valley was made by great earthquakes," the scientist said.

John heard the man talking. "No," John said. "This valley was made by glaciers—slow-moving rivers of ice. I have seen where the ice made marks on the mountain stone millions of years ago."

The scientist laughed. "You are only a sheepherder. What do you know?"

Others laughed at John, too.

John climbed mountain after mountain. Several years passed. Finally John found what he was looking for—a small glacier! He found another and another.

Then the scientists said, "John Muir is right. Yosemite Valley was made by glaciers."

From the mountaintops, John saw
beautiful forests and meadows,
rivers and lakes. "We must never
lose these wild things!" John
thought to himself

John's friends said, "You should
tell others about these beautiful
places. Then they will want to
save them, too."

John began writing about what
he saw in the wilderness.
He wrote about the whiteness of
winter when snowflakes danced
silently among the tall trees.

He wrote about the brightness
of spring when birds sang and
wild flowers filled the valley
with color. And he wrote about
saucy little chipmunks that
chattered noisily all summer long.

"We are all part of the
wilderness," John wrote. "And
the wilderness is part of us."
Many people read John's stories.
He became famous.

But there were people who did not
care about the wilderness. There
were miners who wanted to dig up
all the land looking for gold.

There were sheepherders and
cattlemen who wanted to let their
animals eat all the grass.

There were selfish businessmen
who wanted to build stores
anywhere. "Buildings and roads
are more important than mountains!"
they said.

And there were careless lumber-
men who wanted to cut down all the
tall trees in Yosemite Valley.

"No, no!" John said. "Yosemite must be made a special place to be saved forever!"

John and his friends worked hard to make Yosemite a park for everyone.

Theodore Roosevelt, President of the United States, came to see Yosemite. The people with the President wanted him to stay in a big hotel.

John met the President. "You can't see the wilderness in a hotel," John said. "Come with me."

They walked among the tall trees.
They climbed one of the great
stone mountains. That night John
and the President slept on the
ground under the stars. The
President saw many beautiful
things. He helped make Yosemite a
national park for everyone.

John and his friends formed the
Sierra Club to help save other
wild places. John became its first
president.

John traveled to many places so
he could write about them.

One time when John was in Alaska
to see the glaciers, a little
black dog followed him wherever

he went. But the dog was not friendly. It stayed away from John. John walked across a huge glacier. The dog followed.

"He's not very friendly," John said. "But he likes to be wild and free, just like me."

Then John lost his way. Soon it was dark and cold. John came to a big crack in the glacier.

He climbed across a narrow bridge
of ice. But the little dog was too
frightened to follow. John climbed
back to help the dog. Then he and
the dog found their way back to
John's camp where his friends were

waiting. After that the little dog
was always friendly to John.

He named the dog Stickeen. The
story John wrote about his
adventure with Stickeen became one
of his most famous stories.

John Muir was happiest when he
could share his love of nature
with others—whether a
President of the United States or
a little black dog.

John was writing a book about Alaska when he died on Christmas Eve in 1914.

Because of people like John Muir, there are still beautiful forests and rivers, meadows and mountains which everyone can enjoy.